AF525878

Master

Resilient

Mindset

Thrive Through Adversity, Transform Challenges Into Opportunities, Build Your Inner Strength, and Be Unstoppable.

Dr Arundhati Hoskeri

Master Resilient Mindset

Thrive Through Adversity, Transform Challenges Into Opportunities, Build Your Inner Strength, and Be Unstoppable.

Publication: April 2024

All Rights Reserved

Copyright @ Dr Arundhati Hoskeri

No part of this publication can be reproduced, copied, or transmitted in any form or by any means without the author's permission.

Table of Contents

"Master Resilient Mindset" is the fourth book in **the Cognitive Mastery series.**

"Cognitive Mastery series."

Welcome to the captivating world of the "Cognitive Mastery" book series, where the power of your mind is unlocked, and your potential knows no bounds in exploring essential skills and practices that will revolutionize the way you think, learn, and thrive.

Cognitive mastery refers to the high-level understanding and proficiency in a specific area of knowledge or skill. It involves the ability to effectively integrate and apply information, analyze and solve complex problems, and communicate and articulate ideas clearly. Cognitive mastery is related to the idea of the mental effort required to process information and complete a task. It is important for achieving success in fields such as education, business, and science. With its engaging writing style, practical advice, and actionable strategies, the "Cognitive Mastery" series is your ultimate key to unlocking the potential of your mind and achieving cognitive excellence. Whether you're a student, professional, or lifelong learner, these books will empower you to think smarter, learn faster, and thrive in every aspect of life. So what are you waiting for? Begin your journey to cognitive mastery today!

Overview of the Book

Master Resilient Mindset is the fourth book in the Cognitive Mastery Series.

A resilient mindset is not only about bouncing back from adversity; it's about thriving in the face of challenges and using the lessons learned as stepping stones for growth and success. "Master Resilient Mindset" is a comprehensive guide that equips readers with practical strategies, real-life examples, and insightful reflection questions to cultivate resilience in all areas of life.

Each chapter delves into different aspects of resilience, empowering readers to build inner strength, overcome obstacles, and thrive through challenges.

Chapter 1: What is Resilience?

In this introductory chapter, readers are introduced to the concept of resilience and its significance in handling life's challenges. The chapter begins with an awe-inspiring story of Malavika Hegde, who saved her husband's sinking empire of Café Coffee Day after his untimely demise.

Chapter 2: Resilient Mindset

This chapter explores the key characteristics of a resilient mindset, including optimism, adaptability, and self-efficacy. By understanding the role of mindset in building resilience, readers learn how to overcome adversity with a positive outlook and a belief in their abilities.

Chapter 3: Building Inner Strength

You will explore the strategies for developing inner strength and resilience, beginning with fostering a growth mindset and practicing self-awareness. The book explores techniques for individuals to build emotional resilience and manage stress effectively, including engaging in exercises and activities to strengthen mental and emotional resilience. Through self-reflection and practice, readers learn to cultivate resilience from within.

Chapter 4: Convert Challenges into Opportunities

This chapter explores the benefits of facing adversity and challenges as opportunities for growth and learning. The chapter examines common responses to adversity and guides the cultivation of a positive outlook in difficult situations.

Chapter 5: Overcoming Obstacles

This chapter outlines strategies for overcoming obstacles and setbacks on the path to resilience and practical tips for problem-solving and finding creative solutions to challenges, along with guidance on building resilience through perseverance and determination. By providing practical tips for problem-solving and finding creative solutions to challenges, this chapter empowers you to overcome stumbling blocks and achieve your goals despite setbacks.

Chapter 6: Cultivating Self-Compassion

In this chapter, we explore the significance of self-compassion in building resilience and well-being. Readers learn techniques for practicing self-compassion and self-care, including mindfulness and self-acceptance. It examines the connection between self-compassion and resilience in overcoming life's difficulties, empowering readers to be kind to themselves during difficult times.

Chapter 7: Thriving Through Determination

This chapter examines the long-term benefits of resilience in personal and professional growth. You will explore strategies for thriving in the face of adversity and using resilience as a foundation for success.

It also encourages readers to continue cultivating resilience as an ongoing practice for a fulfilling and meaningful life journey. Through practical exercises, real-life examples, and reflection questions, the book equips readers to thrive through resilience in all aspects of life.

Repeatedly discussing concepts such as mindfulness, self-care, adaptability, and growth mindset in different contexts is aimed at enhancing comprehension of resilience. This approach allows for a more nuanced exploration of how each concept contributes to building resilience and coping with challenges effectively.

"Master Resilient Mindset" is not just a book; it's a step-by-step manual for building resilience and thriving through life's challenges. With practical guidance and inspiring insights, it empowers readers to cultivate a tough mindset, overcome stumbling blocks, and create a life filled with purpose, resilience, and success.

******

About The Author

Dr Arundhati G Hoskeri

MSc, MEd, Ph.D., MA (English), ACTL Diploma in Public Speaking (Trinity College of London)

NDHS (Doctor of Natural Health Sciences)

Certified Cyber Crime Intervention Officer (CCIO)

Educational Consultant for Cambridge International School

Former Director and Principal of Cambridge International School and I B World School

A lifelong learner, Author, Poet, passionate Educator, Counselor, Natural Health Science Expert, Motivational Speaker, and Freelance Journalist.

Dr Arundhati Govind Hoskeri is a remarkable individual whose passion for learning and educational commitments has defined her illustrious journey. With an unquenchable thirst for knowledge, she has obtained master's degrees in three distinct subjects, a testament to her dedication to intellectual growth. Her academic journey culminated in attaining a Ph.D. in Education, reflecting her deep-seated desire to contribute meaningfully to the field.

Throughout her impressive career spanning 37 years, Dr. Arundhati has been a trailblazer in education. Her leadership acumen shines through her role as the head of a prestigious IB (International Baccalaureate) World School and Cambridge International School for over two decades. This extensive experience underscores her exceptional ability to shape and nurture future generations.

Beyond her role as an educator, Dr Arundhati's versatile talents extend into various domains. She is a gifted educator and a practitioner of natural health sciences, earning the title of a Natural Health Science (NDHS) doctor. Her communication prowess is evident in her ACTL Diploma in Public Speaking from Trinity College of London, which has undoubtedly played a pivotal role in her success as a **speaker, educator, and writer.**

Dr Arundhati's impact reaches far beyond the classroom. Her accomplishments as a poet have garnered recognition on national and international platforms, including in countries like India, Sri Lanka, and Malaysia. Her thought-provoking contributions to journalism have graced the pages of esteemed national and international magazines and newspapers, establishing her as a credible voice on various subjects.

As an avid reader and extensive researcher, Dr Arundhati's intellectual curiosity has resulted in the publication of many research articles in esteemed educational journals and conferences—her ability to combine academia with practical insights positions her as **a thought leader** in her field. Her compassion and **dedication to holistic well-being** are evident in her motivational speaker and healer role, where she utilizes her expertise to promote **alternative medicine and positive transformation**.

Accolades and recognition, a testament to her unwavering commitment and exemplary contributions, mark Dr Arundhati's journey. Her presence as a moderator, keynote speaker, and presenter in national and international seminars has solidified her status as a respected voice in various forums. Dr Arundhati lends her expertise as a consultant to upcoming and established Cambridge International School, further impacting the education sector with her wealth of knowledge.

Notably, her journey as an author takes center stage. With a focus on physical health, mental well-being, and the intricate nuances of human behavior, her writing endeavors are a testament to her dedication to empowering individuals with practical insights and actionable advice.

Dr Arundhati Govind Hoskeri's legacy has a profound impact and unwavering dedication. Her multifaceted contributions to education, physical and mental health, writing, and motivational speaking continue to inspire and uplift individuals across the globe, glowing through her accomplishments and sincerity.

She always acknowledges the support of her loving family, especially her husband, Dr Govind N Hoskeri, who has been a driving force behind her success and achievements.

******

The Lady Who Rescued Café Coffee Day from a Massive Debt Closer to One Billion Dollars

In July 2019, India was shocked by the sudden death of VG Siddhartha, the founder of Cafe Coffee Day (CCD), a popular coffee brand loved by millions. His demise not only saddened coffee enthusiasts but also raised concerns about the future of CCD. The company faced a threat to its existence because of a massive debt of Rs 7,000 crore (about one billion USD). Amidst this turmoil, hope emerged as Malavika Hegde, VG Siddhartha's wife. Despite the immense challenge and the void left by her husband's tragic demise, Malavika stepped forward with determination, resilience, and a deep commitment to preserving her husband's legacy and saving the beloved brand.

In **December 2020**, Malavika Hegde took on the role of CEO of Cafe Coffee Day Enterprises Limited (CDEL), the parent company of CCD, by stepping into her husband's shoes. Her primary goal was obvious: to rescue and revive CCD from its financial crisis. The first major hurdle Malavika faced was dealing with the enormous debt. However, she approached the situation with wisdom and courage, aiming not just for survival but for sustainable growth.

She implemented **a series of strategic decisions** to streamline and restructure the company's operations.

- One of her bold strategies was to **avoid** increasing prices for CCD's signature products despite the financial challenges.
- Instead, Malavika focused on downsizing and optimizing operations.
- By making tough decisions to close unprofitable outlets, she ensured efficient allocation of resources.
- Additionally, Malavika Hegde forged strategic partnerships with Blackstone and Shriram Credit Company.
- These partnerships helped reduce expenses and increase revenue streams, contributing significantly to CCD's financial recovery.

By 2021, Malavika's relentless efforts bore fruit, with the company's debt significantly shrinking. By 2023, the debt had reduced to a **manageable Rs 465 crore,** a remarkable achievement considering the initial daunting figure. However, Malavika's leadership goes beyond financial restructuring. She prioritized the **well-being** of CCD's **nearly 25,000 employees**.

During the challenging period, she reassured the workforce, instilling trust and confidence by communicating her commitment to saving the brand and preserving jobs.

Malavika Hegde's journey is a testament to her unwavering dedication to her late husband's dream and a powerful example of how determination can overcome even the most daunting obstacles.

Her strategic decisions, coupled with her empathetic leadership style, not only rescued CCD from financial turmoil but also protected the livelihoods of thousands of employees.

Beyond the business aspect, Malavika's story is a narrative of resilience, leadership, and love for preserving a partner's legacy. Her relentless efforts have reinvigorated CCD, ensuring that it continues to be a beacon for coffee lovers, friends, and professionals alike. She embodies the spirit of resilience and endurance in the face of adversity.

******

Chapter 1: What is Resilience?

"To bear trials with a calm mind robs misfortune of its strength and burden."- Seneca.

Introduction

Life is not always a bed of roses; we encounter some thorns as well. If we focus on the problems and keep brooding on them, we can never solve them. So, instead of focusing on the challenges, we need to find solutions for those challenges.

Resilience refers to the ability to bounce back from challenges, setbacks, and adversity with a positive attitude and determination. It involves developing attitudes, beliefs, and coping strategies that enable individuals to overcome difficult situations and obstacles and emerge stronger and more confident.

Key Characteristics of a Resilience

Optimism

Resilient individuals have an optimistic outlook on life and maintain positivity even during adversity. They believe in their ability to overcome challenges and find solutions.

Adaptability

Resilient individuals are flexible and adaptable. They are open to change and willing to adjust their strategies or plans when faced with unexpected circumstances. Instead of resisting change, they embrace it as an opportunity for growth and learning.

Problem-Solving Skills

Resilient individuals possess strong problem-solving skills. They approach challenges with a proactive attitude, actively seeking solutions and taking decisive actions to address problems effectively. They view obstacles as temporary hurdles to be overcome rather than insurmountable barriers.

Emotional Regulation

Resilient individuals can regulate their emotions effectively. They acknowledge and process their feelings healthily, but they don't allow negative emotions to overwhelm them. Instead, they maintain an emotional balance and focus on productive coping strategies.

Self-Efficacy

Resilient individuals have a strong sense of self-efficacy or belief in their abilities to succeed. They trust in their capacity to overcome challenges and achieve their goals through effort and perseverance. This self-confidence fuels their resilience and motivates them to keep moving forward despite setbacks.

Social Support

People with resilience recognize the importance of social support networks and seek connections with others who can provide encouragement, guidance, and help during difficult times. They are also willing to offer support to others in need, fostering reciprocal relationships that strengthen resilience.

Cultivate a Mindset Leading to Growth

Convert challenges to opportunities for growth and learning. Focus on continuous improvement and believe in developing new skills to overcome obstacles.

Self-Compassion

During difficult times, you need to be kind to yourself. Treat yourself with the same compassion and empathy that you would show to a relative / friend facing similar challenges.

Build Coping Skills

Developing healthy coping mechanisms is crucial for managing stress and adversity. It could include mindfulness, relaxation techniques, exercise, or creative outlets like art or journaling.

Set Realistic Goals

Break larger goals into smaller, achievable steps. Celebrate progress along the way, and don't be discouraged by setbacks. Use every setback and backlash as a learning opportunity to approach the problems differently and keep moving ahead.

Seek Support

Reach out to friends, family, mentors, or mental health professionals for support when needed. Feel free to ask for help or guidance when facing challenges that feel overwhelming.

Practice Resilience-Building

Activities like building relationships, taking part in community service, or volunteering help us build resilience. These experiences can foster a sense of purpose and connection, enhancing resilience.

By cultivating a resilient mindset, individuals can navigate life's trials with greater confidence, perseverance, and emotional well-being. It's an ongoing process that requires self-awareness practice, leading to accepting challenges as opportunities for growth.

******

Poor Village Boy Becomes an IPS (Indian Police Service) Officer

Manoj Kumar Sharma's life overflows with love, bravery, togetherness, and trust. Despite facing difficulties in school, he never gave up on his dreams. His biggest dream was to become an IPS officer.

IPS officer Manoj Kumar Sharma was born in 1977 in an ordinary family in a small village called Bilgaon in Madhya Pradesh, India. Manoj faced many challenges in school and exams, not because he lacked intelligence but because he had no resources. Sharma didn't do well in his ninth and tenth grades and struggled in eleventh grade, too. Because he refused to resort to unfair means in his grade 12 board exam, he ended up failing.

He soon realized the importance of studying and that education was the only means to uplift him and his family from poverty. With a lot of hard work, he cleared the 12th-grade exam in the next attempt but could not score well.

He was determined to succeed and moved to Delhi with the dream of becoming an IPS officer by cracking the competitive UPSC examination despite his limitations of fluency in English.

Life was tough. He had to do odd jobs like driving a tempo, sleeping on pavements, and working in libraries to get by. It was during this time that he met Shraddha, who was also working hard to achieve her goals.

Manoj and Shraddha's love story wasn't smooth either. They faced opposition from their families, but their love and unity grew stronger. Shraddha knew supporting Manoj meant taking on a tough challenge. Eventually, their love conquered all obstacles. Manoj passed the UPSC exam with the 121st rank, and Shraddha became an IRS officer in 2007.

Their story is about determination, resilience, love, and the power of never giving up, no matter how tough life gets. Manoj Kumar Sharma's life is an authentic example of how determination and love can lead to success against all odds.

Manoj's life, determination, and the challenges he faced inspired a Bollywood movie called '12th Fail.' The movie beautifully tells the story of his struggles, his love story, and his journey to success.

******

Chapter 2: The Resilience Mindset

"You have power over your mind–not outside events. Realize this, and you will find strength."

–Marcus Aurelius.

Subunits:

- The concept of resilience and its importance in handling life's challenges.
- Exploring the key characteristics of a resilient mindset, such as optimism, adaptability, and self-efficacy.
- Understanding the role of mindset in building resilience and overcoming adversity.

Developing Resilience

Resilience is the inner strength that helps us bounce back when life throws challenges at us. It's all about being strong and adaptable, even when things get really hard. Life is like a roller coaster ride. Sometimes, it's smooth sailing, but other times, it's bumpy and full of twists and turns. Resilience helps us stay on track even when we encounter those bumps and curves.

When you face challenges like failing a test, losing a job, or going through a breakup, resilience helps you keep going instead of giving up. It's the ability to pick yourself up, dust yourself off, and keep moving forward, even when things seem tough.

Resilience isn't about never feeling sad, scared, or stressed. It's normal to have those feelings when life gets tough. But resilience helps you manage those feelings and find ways to cope so they don't knock you down for too long.

Why is resilience important? Well, life is full of ups and downs, and nobody gets a free pass from challenges. However, resilient people are better able to handle those challenges and come out stronger on the other side. They're more likely to bounce back from setbacks, build strong relationships, and achieve their goals. It is like your secret weapon for facing whatever life throws your way, like having a shield that helps protect you from the tough stuff and gives you the strength to keep going, no matter what.

Resilience isn't just about bouncing back from tough times; it's also about growing stronger because of them. When you face challenges and setbacks, you have the opportunity to learn and grow from those experiences. Each obstacle you overcome can teach you valuable lessons about yourself, your strengths, and how to better handle similar situations in the future.

For example, imagine you're trying out for a sports team, and you need help to succeed. Instead of giving up on your dream of playing sports, you might use that experience to work harder, improve your skills, and try out again next year. By doing so, you not only demonstrate resilience by not letting rejection defeat you, but you also become a better athlete in the process.

Resilience also plays a crucial role in our mental and emotional well-being. When we face tough times, it's natural to feel stressed, anxious, or even overwhelmed. But being resilient means finding healthy ways to cope with those feelings, whether it's talking to a friend, practicing mindfulness, or engaging in activities that bring us joy.

Resilient individuals have stronger support networks. They're more likely to reach out to friends, family, or mentors for help and guidance during difficult times. Having a support system can provide us with the encouragement and perspective we need to navigate challenges effectively.

In today's fast-paced world, where change is constant and unexpected events can arise at any moment, resilience is more important than ever. Whether it's adapting to a new job, dealing with a health crisis, or facing global challenges like the COVID-19 pandemic, resilient individuals are better equipped to weather the storms and emerge stronger on the other side. Resilience is a fundamental life skill that empowers us to overcome obstacles, grow from adversity, and live more fulfilling lives. By cultivating resilience, we can face life's challenges with courage, strength, and optimism, knowing that we have the inner resources to thrive, no matter what comes our way.

Exploring the Key Concepts of a Resilient Mindset

Resilience is like having a sturdy ship that sails through stormy seas, staying afloat no matter how rough the waters get. But what makes some people resilient while others struggle to stay above water? It's all about mindset—the way we think, feel, and respond to life's challenges. Let's explore the key characteristics of a resilient mindset: optimism, adaptability, and self-efficacy.

Optimism

Optimism is like a bright light that shines even in the darkest of times. It's the belief that things will get better, even when everything seems bleak. Optimistic people see setbacks as temporary and setbacks as opportunities for growth.

Imagine you're studying for a test, and you don't do as well as you hoped. Instead of thinking, "I'm a failure," an optimistic mindset says, "I can learn from this and do better next time." It's about focusing on solutions rather than dwelling on problems. Optimism doesn't mean ignoring reality or pretending everything is fine when it's not. It's about finding the silver lining in a dark cloud and maintaining a positive outlook, even in challenging circumstances.

Adaptability

Adaptability is the ability to bend without breaking, like a sturdy tree swaying in the wind. It's about being flexible and open to change, even when it's unexpected or uncomfortable. Adaptability allows us to adjust our plans and behaviors in response to new situations or obstacles.

Life is full of twists and turns, and things don't always go according to plan. But resilient individuals can roll with the punches and adapt to whatever comes their way. They're like skilled improvisers, making the best of whatever hand they're dealt.

For example, imagine you're working on a group project, and a team member drops out at the last minute. Instead of panicking or giving up an adaptable mindset says, "Let's brainstorm new ideas and figure out how to make this work." It's about being resourceful and finding creative solutions to unexpected challenges.

Self-Efficacy

Self-efficacy is like having a deep well of confidence and belief in your abilities. It's the belief that you have the power to influence your outcomes and achieve your goals, even in the face of adversity. People with high self-efficacy trust in their skills and capabilities, which empowers them to take on challenges with courage and determination.

Imagine you're starting a new job in an unfamiliar field. Instead of feeling overwhelmed or doubting yourself, a strong sense of self-efficacy says, "I may not know everything now, but I can learn and grow." It's about having faith in your capacity to succeed, even when the path ahead seems daunting.

Experience and accomplishment nurture self-efficacy. Each time we overcome a challenge or achieve a goal, our confidence grows stronger, reinforcing our belief in our abilities.

In summary, optimism, adaptability, and self-efficacy characterize a resilient mindset. These key traits empower us to face life's challenges with courage, resilience, and determination. By cultivating these qualities within ourselves, we can build a solid foundation for thriving in the face of adversity and living our best lives.

Building Resilience to Overcome Adversity

Life presents us with trials that can sometimes leave us feeling shaken and uncertain. But what if I told you that the way we think and perceive challenges can make all the difference? That's where mindset comes in.

Let's explore how our mindset shapes our ability to build resilience and overcome adversity.

The Power of Perspective

Our mindset is like the lens through which we view the world. It influences how we interpret events, how we feel about ourselves, and how we respond to challenges. A positive mindset can help us see setbacks as opportunities for growth, while a negative mindset may lead us to feel defeated and hopeless.

For example, imagine you face a difficult situation, like losing your job. A positive mindset might say,

- "This is a chance for me to explore new career opportunities and discover what truly fulfills me.

A negative mindset might say,

- "I'll never find another job, and I'm doomed to fail."

By choosing to adopt a positive perspective, we can reframe challenges as stepping stones rather than stumbling blocks. This shift in mindset can fuel our resilience and give us the strength to persevere in the face of adversity.

The Role of Belief

Our beliefs about our strengths, weaknesses, and abilities shape our resilience.

If we believe in our capacity to overcome obstacles and achieve our goals, we're more likely to bounce back from setbacks with determination and perseverance.

Self-efficacy refers to this belief in our abilities. It's like having an inner reservoir of confidence and resilience that empowers us to tackle challenges head-on.

For example, imagine you face a task like giving a presentation in front of a large audience. If you believe in your ability to communicate effectively and handle pressure, you're more likely to approach the task with confidence and poise. But if you doubt your abilities and fear failure, you may struggle to perform at your best.

By fostering self-belief and adopting a mindset focused on growth, we can enhance our ability to bounce back from setbacks and tackle difficulties with confidence and determination.

The Importance of Adaptability

Resilience is the ability to bounce back from hardship and grow stronger. Our ability to adapt to change and handle uncertainty plays a crucial role in building resilience.

Life is unpredictable, and things sometimes go differently than planned. However, resilient individuals can roll with the punches and adjust their course when faced with unexpected challenges.

Adaptability is like a muscle—the more we exercise it, the stronger it becomes. By embracing change and deciding to step outside our routine tasks and comfort zones, we can develop the flexibility and resilience needed to thrive in an ever-changing world.

For example, imagine you're facing a sudden change in your personal life, like a breakup or a relocation. Instead of clinging to the familiar and resisting change, an adaptable mindset says, "I may not have control over this situation, but I can choose how I respond to it." By accepting change and adapting, we can emerge stronger and more resilient than before.

Cultivating Resilience Through Mindfulness

Mindfulness is another powerful tool for overcoming adversity. By practicing mindfulness, the art of being present and fully engaged at the moment, we develop clarity in our thinking and remain calm and balanced, which helps us tide over difficult situations with the right approach.

Mindfulness equips us to be non-judgmental and helps us observe our thoughts and emotions calmly, allowing us to respond to adversity with greater wisdom and compassion. Instead of getting swept away by negative thoughts and emotions, we can choose to cultivate a mindset of acceptance and resilience.

For example, imagine you're facing a stressful situation, like a tight deadline at work or a conflict with a loved one. Instead of reacting impulsively or getting caught up in worry and fear, mindfulness encourages us to pause, ponder, take a deep breath, and respond thoughtfully rather than impulsively. Integrating mindfulness into our daily lives helps us develop greater emotional balance, inner strength, and a deeper sense of well-being. Our mindset plays a powerful role in building resilience and overcoming adversity. By cultivating a positive perspective, nurturing our self-belief and adaptability, and practicing mindfulness, we become more resilient to face tough situations and challenges.

Practical exercises and reflection questions will help you apply the principles of resilience to your lives.

Practical Exercises

Positive Affirmations

Prepare a list of positive affirmations that resonate with you, such as:

- "I can overcome challenges."
- "I embrace change and adapt with resilience."
- "I am calm and composed, and I respond to situations rather than react impulsively."

Repeat these affirmations daily, especially during moments of difficulty or self-doubt.

Mindfulness Meditation

Practice a mindfulness meditation exercise, focusing on deep breathing and awareness of the present moment.

Please refer to the script at the end of this chapter. Read it 3-4 times and then record it in your voice and listen to it daily before going to bed and as soon as you get up. It works like magic. Please do it for 45 days without a break and experience the results.

Practice mindfulness regularly to cultivate a calm and resilient mindset.

Writing in a journal encourages a mindset of personal growth.

Journaling is the best way to label your feelings and reflect on the situations to seek answers. Honestly, jot down your challenges, setbacks, and successes and reflect.

Identify lessons learned, strengths gained, and areas for growth in each experience.

Reflection Questions:

1. **Reflect on a recent challenge or setback you've faced.**

- How did you respond to the situation?
- Did you approach it with a resilience mindset, or did you struggle with feelings of defeat or helplessness?

2. **Consider a role model or inspirational figure known for their resilience.**

- What qualities or characteristics do they embody you to admire?
- How can you incorporate these traits into your own life and mindset?

3. **Think about a time when you achieved success despite facing obstacles.**

- What strengths or resources did you draw upon to overcome adversity?
- How can you apply these lessons to future challenges?

4. **Consider areas of your life where you may struggle with a fixed mindset or negative self-talk.**

Reflect on how you can shift towards a growth mindset and cultivate more resilience in these areas.

5. **Identify one small step you can take today to cultivate a resilient mindset.**

- It could be practicing self-compassion, setting realistic goals, or seeking support from others.
- How can you commit to incorporating this practice into your daily life?

By incorporating these practical exercises and reflection questions, you can engage with the material on a deeper level and begin effectively applying resilience principles to your own lives. Through self-reflection, practice, and inspiration from real-life stories, you can cultivate a resilient mindset that empowers you to thrive in the face of adversity.

*****

Chapter 3: Building Inner Strength

"In the depth of winter,

I finally learned that within me,

there lay an invincible summer."

–Albert Camus.

Subunits:

- Strategies for developing inner strength.
- Techniques for building emotional balance and managing stress.
- Exercises and activities to strengthen mental and emotional resilience.

Strategies for Developing Inner Strength

Life can be tough sometimes, with challenges and setbacks that can leave us feeling overwhelmed and uncertain. But the good news is that we all can develop inner strength and resilience, which is the ability to bounce back from adversity and thrive in the face of challenges.

Let's explore some simple yet powerful strategies for building resilience and fostering inner strength.

Fostering a Growth Mindset

One of the most powerful tools for building resilience is cultivating a growth mindset. Believing in the power of effort, learning, and perseverance, we cultivate a growth mindset to develop our abilities and intelligence. Instead of viewing challenges as threats to our self-worth, those with a growth mindset see them as opportunities for growth and learning.

So, how can you foster a growth mindset? Start by reframing challenges as opportunities for growth rather than obstacles to be avoided. When faced with a setback or failure, ask yourself: What can I learn from this experience? How can I use this as an opportunity to improve and grow?

Another key aspect of fostering a growth mindset is embracing the power of "yet."

Instead of saying, "I can't do this," add the word **"yet"** to the end of your statement: **"I can't do this yet."** This simple shift in language can open up possibilities and encourage perseverance in the face of obstacles.

By adopting a growth mindset, you can build resilience and develop the inner strength needed to overcome adversity and achieve your goals.

Practicing Self-Awareness

Self-awareness is another essential skill for building resilience and inner strength. It is about being mindful of your thoughts, emotions, and reactions to different situations, as well as understanding your strengths, weaknesses, and values.

One way to cultivate self-awareness is through mindfulness practices, such as meditation, deep breathing, or journaling. These practices can help you become more attuned to your inner experiences and develop greater clarity and insight into your thoughts and emotions.

Another helpful strategy for practicing self-awareness is reflection. Spare time to reflect on your positive and negative experiences and consider how they have shaped you as a person. What have you learned about yourself? What strengths have you developed? What areas could you improve upon?

By cultivating self-awareness, you can better understand your own needs, motivations, and values, which can help you navigate challenges with greater resilience and inner strength.

Building a Support Network

Building a strong support network is another important strategy for developing resilience and inner strength. Surrounding yourself with supportive friends, family members, mentors, and colleagues can provide you with the encouragement, guidance, and perspective you need to effectively navigate life's challenges.

Reach out to trusted individuals in your life when you're facing difficulties, and don't be afraid to ask for help or seek support. Having a supportive network of people who care about you can help you feel less alone and more resilient in the face of adversity. Besides seeking support from others, it's also important to be supportive of yourself. Practice self-compassion and self-care, and remind yourself that it's okay to ask for help when you need it. Be kind to yourself, especially during difficult times.

Cultivating Resilience Through Action

Finally, one of the most effective ways to develop resilience and inner strength is through action. Take proactive steps to face your fears, overcome obstacles, and pursue your goals, even when it feels challenging or intimidating.

Set realistic goals for yourself, map out manageable steps, and take consistent action toward achieving them. Celebrate your progress along the way, and don't be discouraged by setbacks or failures–they're all part of the learning process.

Practice resilience-building skills, such as problem-solving, decision-making, and emotion regulation, in your daily life. Identify opportunities to challenge yourself and step outside of your comfort zone, knowing that each experience is there to help you grow stronger and more resilient.

By actively working on developing a positive mindset, being aware of yourself, building a support system, and being resilient through taking action, you can strengthen yourself internally to overcome challenges and succeed in life.

Remember, resilience is not about being perfect or never experiencing difficulties – it's about bouncing back stronger and more resilient than before, no matter what life throws your way.

Techniques For Building Emotional Strength

Life can throw us curveballs sometimes, leaving us feeling stressed, anxious, or overwhelmed. But the good news is that we can build emotional resilience–the ability to bounce back from adversity and cope with life's challenges healthily. Let's explore some simple yet powerful techniques for building emotional resilience and managing stress effectively.

Practice Mindfulness and Relaxation Techniques

Mindfulness is nothing but an effective way to reduce stress and build emotional resilience. It involves paying attention to the present moment without judgment, which can help us stay grounded and calm, even in difficult situations.

One way to practice mindfulness is through deep breathing exercises. Take a few minutes each day to bring awareness to your breath by inhaling through your nose and exhaling slowly through your mouth. Notice how your body feels as you breathe, and allow yourself to relax with each breath.

PMT, or progressive muscle relaxation, involves tensing and then relaxing different muscle groups in your body. Start by tensing your muscles tightly for a few seconds, then release and relax them completely. Move from one muscle group to the next, working your way through your body from head to toe.

For example, imagine you're feeling stressed about an upcoming exam or an interview. You could take a few minutes to practice abdominal breathing exercises or progressive muscle relaxation techniques to calm your nerves and focus your mind.

Develop Healthy Coping Strategies

When faced with stress or adversity, healthy coping strategies help you manage your emotions and stay resilient. Instead of giving in to unhealthy habits like overeating, substance abuse, or avoidance, try to develop positive coping strategies that promote emotional well-being.

One effective coping strategy is journaling. Jotting down your feelings can help you process difficult emotions, gain perspective on challenging situations, and identify potential solutions. Try setting aside a few minutes each day to journal about your experiences, thoughts, and emotions.

Another healthy coping strategy is indulging in joyful activities, such as spending time with pets, going for a walk in nature, or pursuing a hobby you enjoy. Find activities that help you unwind and recharge your batteries.

For example, imagine you need more time to feel overwhelmed with work or school responsibilities. Instead of pushing yourself to the brink of burnout, you could take a break to go for a walk outside or spend time with friends to recharge your batteries and gain a fresh perspective on your situation.

Build a Strong Support Network

Having a strong support network of friends, family members, and other trusted individuals can provide a valuable source of emotional support and encouragement during difficult times. Reach out to your support network when you're feeling stressed or overwhelmed, and don't be afraid to ask for help if you need it.

For example, imagine you're going through a tough breakup or experiencing a family conflict. Instead of trying to deal with your emotions alone, seek support from a trusted friend or family member. Talking your heart out to your trusted ones makes you feel lighter and gives a sense of security that there is someone with whom you can unburden.

Practice Self-Care

Self-care is essential for building emotional resilience and managing stress effectively. It is about taking care of your physical, emotional, and mental well-being by prioritizing activities that nourish and replenish your body and mind.

Make time for activities that promote self-care, such as getting enough sleep, exercising regularly, eating a balanced diet, and engaging in hobbies and activities that bring you joy and relaxation. Set aside time each day to do something for yourself, whether it's taking a relaxed bath or pursuing a hobby you enjoy. For example, imagine you're feeling burned out from work or school. Instead of pushing yourself to keep going, take a step back and prioritize self-care activities that help you replenish your energy levels.

Building emotional resilience and managing stress involves practicing mindfulness and relaxation techniques, developing healthy coping strategies and a strong support network, and prioritizing self-care. By incorporating these techniques into your daily life, you can strengthen your resilience and better cope with life's challenges, no matter what comes your way. Remember, resilience is not about avoiding stress altogether–it's about learning how to bounce back stronger and more resilient than before, even in the face of adversity.

Exercises to Strengthen Mind

Life can be like a rollercoaster, with its ups and downs that sometimes leave us feeling overwhelmed or stressed. But just like a muscle, we can strengthen our mental and emotional resilience—the ability to bounce back from challenges and keep going with a positive outlook. Let's explore some exercises and activities that can help us build this resilience in simple and practical ways.

Gratitude Practice

Gratitude is a powerful tool for developing mental and emotional resilience. It involves taking time each day to reflect on the things we're thankful for, no matter how big or small. A positive mindset can shift our thoughts from scarcity to abundance.

Maintaining a gratitude journal is the best way to thank the universe. Every day, write down five things you're grateful for. It could be a simple thing like a beautiful sunrise you witnessed, a loving gesture from a friend, a delicious meal at home, or the emotional support of a family member. Such regular practice can train your brain to focus on the good things in life, even when times are tough.

For example, imagine you're feeling stressed about work or school. Taking a few minutes to write down things you're grateful for can help shift your perspective and make you focus on the positive aspects of your life, even amidst challenges.

Mindfulness Meditation

Mindfulness meditation is another powerful exercise for strengthening mental and emotional resilience. It is about being in the present moment without being judgmental, allowing us to observe our thoughts and emotions with greater clarity and calmness.

Look for a quiet and comfortable space where you won't be disturbed to practice mindfulness meditation. Please close your eyes and breathe in slowly, focusing on the sensation of fresh air as it enters and leaves your body. Please note any thoughts or emotions that may arise without trying to change or judge them, and allow them to pass like clouds in the sky.

For example, when you're feeling anxious or overwhelmed, taking a few minutes to practice mindfulness can reduce stress and calm your mind, allowing you to face challenges with greater clarity and resilience.

Positive Affirmations

Positive affirmations are simple statements that can help boost self-confidence and promote a positive mindset. By repeating these affirmations regularly, we can train our brains to focus on our strengths and capabilities rather than on our shortcomings or limitations.

Choose some positive affirmations that resonate with you, such as

- "I am strong and capable," "I deserve happiness and success," or
- "I am resilient and can overcome any challenge."

Repeat these affirmations to yourself regularly, especially when you're feeling stressed or doubtful.

For example, imagine you're facing an arduous task. Repeating affirmations like:

- "I am perfectly capable of handling this challenge," or
- "I have the skills and resources to succeed. "

can help boost your confidence and resilience, allowing you to tackle the task with a positive mindset.

Physical Exercise

Physical exercise isn't just good for our bodies–it's also great for our mental and emotional well-being. Regular exercise releases endorphins–chemicals in the brain that act as natural mood lifters–helping to reduce stress and boost feelings of happiness and resilience.

Make an exercise routine that you enjoy, whether it's jogging, walking, cycling, swimming, dancing, aerobics or practicing yoga. Work out for at least forty minutes of moderate-intensity exercise four to five times a week to get the mental and emotional benefits.

For example, imagine you're feeling overwhelmed with work or school. Taking a break to go for a walk or jog can help clear your mind, reduce stress, and boost your resilience, letting you return to your tasks with renewed energy and enhanced focus.

Creative Expression

Engaging yourself in creative activities is a powerful way to strengthen mental and emotional resilience. Whether it's painting, drawing, writing, dancing, or playing music, creative expression allows us to channel our emotions positively and constructively, helping us process difficult experiences and find meaning and purpose in life.

For example, imagine you're feeling sad or anxious. Taking some time to write in a journal, paint a picture, or play an instrument can help you express and release your emotions, providing a sense of catharsis and promoting emotional resilience.

In summary, exercises and activities like gratitude practice, mindfulness meditation, positive affirmations, physical exercise, and creative expression can all help strengthen mental and emotional resilience. By adopting such practices into your daily life, you can build the inner strength and resilience needed to navigate life's challenges with grace and positivity, no matter what comes your way. Remember, resilience is not about never experiencing difficulties–it's about learning how to bounce back stronger and more resilient than before, even in the face of adversity.

Time to Reflect

I. Reflect on a recent challenging situation that triggered stress or negative emotions. How did you respond to the situation? Were you able to maintain a growth mindset and practice self-awareness in the face of adversity?

II. Consider a time when you felt emotionally overwhelmed or drained. What strategies did you use to manage stress and build resilience? How effective were these techniques in helping you cope with difficult emotions?

III. Think about activities or hobbies that bring you joy and relaxation. How can you incorporate more of these activities into your daily routine to strengthen your mental and emotional resilience?

IV. Reflect on your self-talk and inner dialogue during challenging times. Are you practicing self-compassion and fostering a growth mindset, or are you being self-critical and fixed in your thinking? How can you cultivate a more resilient mindset moving forward?

V. Consider seeking support from a therapist, counselor, or support group if you're struggling to manage stress or build resilience on your own. How can you focus on maintaining your mental and emotional balance and actively address any difficulties you're encountering?

By incorporating these practical exercises, real-life examples, and reflection questions into Chapter 2: Building Inner Strength, readers can deepen their understanding of resilience principles and apply them to their own lives effectively. Through self-awareness, stress management techniques, and engaging in activities that promote resilience, they can strengthen their inner resilience and thrive in the face of life's challenges.

*****

Integrity and Determination are Essential for Leadership

Lal Bahadur Shastri, one of the most respected former Prime Minister of India, is indeed a classic example of resilience and determination in the face of adversity. Born on October 2, 1904, in a humble family in Mughalsarai, Uttar Pradesh, Shastri faced many challenges and hardships throughout his life.

Early Life and Education

Growing up in poverty, Shastri's family struggled to make ends meet. Despite the financial constraints, he was determined to receive an education. He had to cross a river every day by swimming with his only pair of clothes secured on his head to reach the school. He faced challenges, such as a lack of resources, but his perseverance led him to complete his schooling and later pursue higher education at the Kashi Vidyapeeth in Varanasi.

Entry into Politics

Shastri's entry into politics during the Indian independence movement showcased his resilience and commitment to serving the nation. He actively took part in several freedom movements and protests against British colonial rule, demonstrating his unwavering dedication to the cause of freedom.

Adaptation and Leadership

Shastri's ability to adapt and lead became evident during his tenure as a prominent leader in independent India. He held several key positions in the government, including Minister of Railways and Minister of Home Affairs. His pragmatic approach to governance and focus on addressing the needs of the common people earned him respect and admiration across the nation.

Challenges and Adversity

One of the most challenging periods in Shastri's career came during the Indo-Pakistani War of 1965. As Prime Minister, he faced immense pressure and adversity while leading the country through a critical military conflict. Despite the odds stacked against India, Shastri's resilience and steadfast leadership inspired the nation to unite and face the challenges head-on.

"Jai Jawan Jai Kisan"

Shastri's famous slogan "Jai Jawan Jai Kisan" (Hail the Soldier, Hail the Farmer) exemplified his empathy for the soldiers defending the country's borders and his concern for the welfare of farmers. This motto became a rallying cry for national unity and resilience during testing times.

Legacy of Integrity

Throughout his career, Lal Bahadur Shastri was known for his integrity, humility, and dedication to public service. His simple lifestyle and ethical leadership left a lasting impact on Indian politics and society.

Ultimate Success

Despite the challenges he faced, Shastri's resilience and determination ultimately led to significant achievements, including diplomatic successes during his tenure as Prime Minister, such as the Tashkent Agreement that brought an end to the Indo-Pakistani War.

Lal Bahadur Shastri's life is a testament to the power of resilience, adaptability, and persistence in the face of adversity. His journey from poor and humble beginnings to becoming a revered leader of India serves as an inspiration for generations to come, highlighting the importance of staying true to one's values and never giving up, no matter how daunting the obstacles may seem.

******

Chapter 4: Overcoming Obstacles

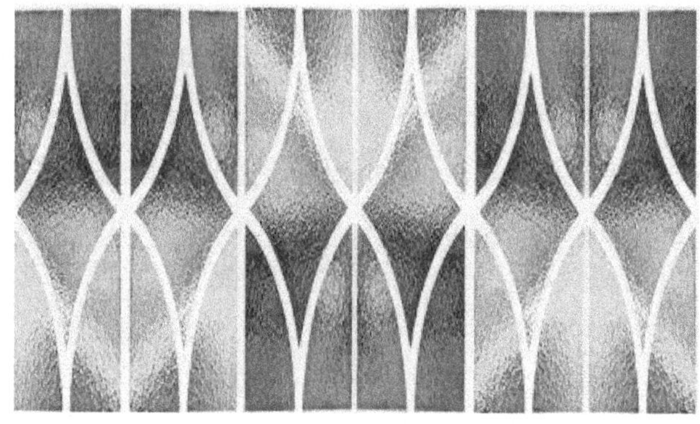

"People are like stained-glass windows.
They sparkle and shine when the sun is out,
but when the darkness sets in, their true
beauty is
revealed only if there is a light from within."
— Elisabeth Kubler-Ross

Subunits

- Strategies for overcoming obstacles and setbacks.
- Practical tips for problem-solving and finding creative solutions to challenges.
- Guidance in building resilience through perseverance and determination.

Strategies for Overcoming Obstacles

Life may be full of setbacks, challenges, and obstacles that can sometimes be annihilating. But with the right mindset and strategies, we can face these difficulties and emerge stronger and more resilient than before. Effective strategies for overcoming obstacles and setbacks on the path to resilience help us bounce back.

Develop a Growth Mindset

Cultivating a mindset focused on growth is crucial for developing resilience. Instead of viewing challenges as insurmountable obstacles, see them as opportunities for growth and learning. Believe that you can improve your skills and abilities through effort and perseverance.

The minute we focus only on the problem and mull over it, we get affected emotionally, which may fog our thinking. So, immediately shifting our brain towards finding solutions once the problem is noted or identified is like winning the battle halfway. Instead of giving up when faced with an uphill task, approach it with the mindset that you can learn and grow from the experience, regardless of the outcome. Focus on your actions and put in your best efforts, and the results will follow.

Practice Self-Compassion

Often, we are harsh to ourselves and either pass the blame on others or blame ourselves and feel inadequate. The guilty mindset fanned by self-blame will not solve any problem. Be kind to yourself during difficult times and treat yourself with the same compassion and understanding you would offer to a friend. Acknowledge your feelings without judgment and remind yourself that it's okay to struggle sometimes.

Instead of criticizing yourself for making a mistake, offer yourself words of encouragement and remind yourself that everyone makes mistakes.

Build a Strong Support Network

Man is a social being; we live in a society, and we constantly need support from others in small or big ways. So, surround yourself with supportive friends, family members, and mentors who can offer encouragement, guidance, and perspective during challenging times.

Reach out to your support network when you need help or reassurance. Please seek advice from a trusted friend or family member when facing a tough decision or situation, and lean on them for emotional support.

Set Sensible Goals

Set achievable goals and arrange them into smaller, manageable steps. Celebrate your successes, however small they may seem, and adjust your goals as needed based on your circumstances and priorities. Instead of setting a lofty goal to overhaul your diet and exercise routine completely overnight, take small steps by changing your daily habits.

While setting a short-term or long-term goal, write down certain important factors like availability of time and other resources, then strategize and prioritize the tasks to reach your goal.

Practice Mindfulness

Mindfulness is nothing but paying attention to the present moment without judgment and becoming aware and accepting of your thoughts, emotions, and experiences. You can practice mindfulness through meditation, deep breathing, or simply taking a few moments to pause and observe your surroundings.

Please take a few minutes each day to practice mindful breathing. Keep focusing on your breath as it enters and leaves your body.

Develop Problem-Solving Skills

When faced with challenges and setbacks, take a proactive approach and find practical ways to overcome them. Break down problems into smaller, more manageable tasks, and brainstorm potential solutions with an open mind.

Instead of feeling overwhelmed by a complex problem, break it down into smaller steps and take each one systematically, seeking help or resources as needed.

Cultivate optimism

Keep a positive outlook and focus on the potential for growth and improvement, even in the face of adversity. Practice reframing negative thoughts into more positive and empowering ones, and surround yourself with uplifting and optimistic influences. Instead of brooding over past failures, focus on the lessons learned and identify the opportunities for growth and improvement.

Practice gratitude

Take time each day to reflect on the things you're thankful for, no matter how big or small. Cultivating an attitude of gratitude can help shift your focus away from negativity and toward the positive aspects of your life. Keep a gratitude journal and write down three things you're grateful for each day, whether it's a breath of fresh air, your loving family, beautiful nature, a kind gesture from a friend, or a delicious meal you had.

Take Care of Yourself

Prioritize self-care and make time for activities that nourish your body, mind, and soul. Get enough sleep, eat a balanced diet, exercise regularly, and engage in activities that bring you joy and relaxation. Set aside time each week for activities that help you recharge and unwind, whether it's going for a walk in nature, practicing yoga, or spending time with loved ones.

Foster Flexibility

Remain flexible and adaptable in the face of change, and be willing to adjust your plans and expectations as needed. Embrace uncertainty as a natural part of life and focus on finding creative solutions to unexpected challenges. Instead of becoming rigid and resistant to change, approach new situations with an open mind and a willingness to adapt and learn.

Learn from Failure

View failure as an opportunity for growing and learning some lessons rather than a reflection of your worth or abilities. Embrace the lessons learned from setbacks and mistakes and use them to inform future decisions and actions. Instead of giving up after experiencing a setback, find out what went wrong and how you can improve next time, then adjust your approach accordingly.

Maintain perspective

Keep challenges and setbacks in perspective by focusing on the bigger picture and recognizing that difficulties are a temporary part of the human experience. Cultivate resilience by maintaining a sense of humor, finding purpose in difficult situations, and staying connected to your values and beliefs. When faced with a difficult situation, remind yourself that **it's just one small chapter in the larger story of your life and that you have the strength and resilience to overcome it.**

Conquering challenges and setbacks on the path to resilience requires a combination of mindset, skills, and strategies. With a growth mindset, practicing self-compassion, building a strong support network, setting realistic goals, practicing mindfulness, developing problem-solving skills, cultivating optimism, practicing gratitude, taking care of yourself, fostering flexibility, learning from failure, and maintaining perspective, you can overcome life's challenges with grace. Resilience is not about avoiding difficulties–it's about facing them head-on with courage and determination, knowing that you have the inner resources to overcome them and emerge stronger than before.

Practical Tips for Problem-Solving and Finding Creative Solutions to Challenges

Define the Problem Clearly

Before you can solve a problem, you need to understand it. Take the time to define the problem you're facing clearly, including any underlying issues or root causes that may contribute to it.

If you need help to meet a deadline at work, the problem may be a lack of time management skills, unclear priorities, or unexpected obstacles that have arisen.

Break the Problem Down into Smaller Steps

If you want to trek a mountain, you need to take that first step to climb rather than looking at it again and again from top to bottom and worrying about it.

Big problems can feel overwhelming, but breaking them down into more manageable and smaller steps can make them easier to tackle. Identify the individual components of the problem and prioritize them based on their importance and urgency.

If you're overwhelmed by the prospect of planning a major event, break the task down into smaller steps, like creating a guest list, choosing a venue, and setting a budget.

Brainstorm Potential Solutions

Once you understand the problem, brainstorm potential solutions without judgment or criticism. Be creative and open-minded, considering all possible options, no matter how unconventional they may seem.

If you're trying to increase sales for your business, brainstorm potential marketing strategies, such as social media campaigns, email newsletters, or partnerships with other businesses.

Consider Multiple Perspectives

Seek input from others who may have different perspectives or experiences that could offer valuable insights into the problem. Consider consulting colleagues, friends, mentors, or experts in the field for their input and advice.

If you're struggling to resolve a conflict with a coworker, seek input from other team members or a trusted mentor who can offer a different perspective on the situation.

Evaluate the Pros and Cons

Once you have a list of potential solutions, consider the pros and cons of each option to determine which one is most likely to address the problem effectively. Consider factors like feasibility, cost, time investment, and potential risks or drawbacks.

For example, if you're considering two different job offers, write them down and reflect on the pros and cons of each opportunity based on factors like salary, benefits, job responsibilities, and opportunities for advancement. Try to get some insight into people working in those organizations and learn about the work culture.

Experiment and Iterate

Feel free to experiment with different solutions and approaches to see what works best. Be willing to adapt and iterate as needed based on feedback and results, refining your approach over time to achieve the desired outcome.

Example: If you're trying to improve your productivity, experiment with different time management techniques like the **Pomodoro Technique** or task batching to see which one helps you stay focused and organized.

Treat Failure as a Teacher

Failure is a natural part of the problem-solving process, and it's important to learn from your mistakes and setbacks rather than letting them discourage you. Use every failure as an opportunity to learn something new, grow, and apply the lessons learned to future problem-solving efforts.

Example: If a marketing campaign doesn't generate the expected results, analyze what went wrong and why, and use that information to reframe future marketing strategies.

Stay Flexible

Be flexible and adjust your approach as needed based on changing circumstances or new information that arises. Keep an open mind and be prepared to pivot if necessary to find a solution that works.

Example: If unexpected obstacles arise while planning an event, be prepared to adapt and adjust your plans accordingly to ensure the event's success.

Seek Feedback and Input

Seek feedback and input from others throughout the problem-solving process. Solicit feedback from colleagues, mentors, or stakeholders to get valuable insights and perspectives on the problem and potential solutions.

Example: If you're developing a new product, seek input from potential customers through surveys, focus groups, or beta testing to gather feedback on the product's features and functionality.

Stay Positive and Persistent

Keep a positive attitude and believe in your ability to find a solution to the problem, even when faced with obstacles or setbacks. Stay persistent and resilient in your efforts, and keep going until you've achieved your goal.

Example: If you encounter challenges while learning a new skill, stay positive and remind yourself that you can overcome obstacles with time and practice.

Use Visual Tools and Diagrams

Visual tools like flowcharts, diagrams, or mind maps help you understand the problem and potential solutions more clearly. Use these tools to map out the problem-solving process and identify connections between distinct elements.

Example: If you're trying to optimize a workflow, create a flowchart that outlines the steps involved and identifies areas for improvement.

Celebrate Successes and Learn from Them

Celebrate your successes along the way, no matter how small, and use them as motivation to keep moving forward. Take time to reflect on what went well and why, and apply those insights to future problem-solving efforts.

Example: If you successfully launch a new product or service, celebrate the achievement with your team and reflect on the factors that contributed to its success, such as effective collaboration or strategic planning.

In summary, problem-solving is an essential skill for navigating life's challenges and achieving your goals. By following these practical strategies, you can approach problems with confidence, creativity, and resilience, finding innovative solutions that lead to success. Remember, every problem is an opportunity for growth and learning, so embrace challenges with an open mind and a willingness to adapt and evolve.

Building Perseverance and Determination

Building resilience through perseverance and determination is crucial for conquering obstacles and thriving in the face of adversity.

Set Clear Goals

Clarity while setting goals provides a sense of direction and purpose, motivating you to persevere through challenges to achieve your objectives. Break your goals down into smaller, actionable chunks to make them more manageable, and track your progress along the way.

Example. Suppose your goal is to start a small business. Break it down into smaller steps, like

- Conducting market research.
- Writing a business plan.
- Securing funding.
- Launching your product or service.

Develop a Growth Mindset

Cultivate a growth mindset by believing in the development of your abilities and intelligence through dedication and hard work. Treat challenges as opportunities for growth and learning rather than viewing setbacks as failures.

Example: Instead of giving up when faced with a difficult task, approach it with the mindset that you can learn and succeed with effort and perseverance.

Stay Flexible

The willingness to adjust and adapt in response to changing circumstances or unexpected obstacles is crucial for growth. Stay open-minded and resilient, ready to pivot when necessary to march towards your goals.

Example: If your original plan isn't working as expected, be flexible and willing to try new strategies or approaches to achieve the desired outcome.

Cultivate optimism

Maintain a positive outlook in life and focus on the potential for growth and improvement, even in the face of adversity. Practice reframing negative thoughts into more positive and empowering ones, and surround yourself with uplifting influences.

Example: Instead of dwelling on past failures, focus on the lessons learned and the opportunities for growth and improvement that arise from challenging experiences.

Develop Problem-Solving Skills

Develop strong problem-solving skills to navigate obstacles and find creative solutions to challenges effectively. Break problems down into smaller components, brainstorm potential solutions, and evaluate the pros and cons of each option.

Example: When faced with a difficult problem, brainstorm potential solutions and consider the feasibility, cost, and potential risks or drawbacks of each option before making a decision.

Practice Self-Compassion

Be kind to yourself during difficult times and treat yourself with the same compassion and understanding you would offer to a friend. Acknowledge your feelings without judgment and remind yourself that it's okay to struggle sometimes.

Example: Instead of being hard on yourself for making a mistake, offer yourself words of encouragement and remind yourself that everyone makes mistakes.

Build a Strong Support Network

Surround yourself with supportive friends, family members, and mentors who can offer encouragement, guidance, and perspective during challenging times. Lean on your support network for emotional support and practical assistance when needed.

Example: Seek advice from a trusted friend or family member when facing a difficult decision or situation, and rely on them for emotional support during challenging times.

Stay Persistent

Maintain a sense of determination and persistence, refusing to give up in the face of obstacles or setbacks. Remain focused on your goals and keep moving ahead, even when progress is slow or difficult.

Example: Keep working towards your goals, even when faced with setbacks or obstacles. Stay persistent and resilient, knowing that every step forward brings you closer to success.

Learn from Failure

View failure as a natural part of the learning process and a step for growth and improvement. Embrace the lessons learned from setbacks and mistakes and use them to inform future decisions and actions.

Example: If a project doesn't go as planned, reflect on what went wrong and why, and use that information to adjust your approach and improve future outcomes.

Practice gratitude

Take time each day to reflect on the things you're thankful for, no matter how big or small. Cultivating an attitude of gratitude helps you focus on the positive aspects of your life.

Seek inspiration

Find inspiration in the stories of others who have overcome challenges and achieved success through perseverance and determination. Read books and watch documentaries about resilient individuals who have faced adversity with courage and resilience.

Example: Learn about historical figures like Nelson Mandela, who spent 27 years in prison for his activism against apartheid before becoming the first black president of South Africa.

Take Care of Yourself

Prioritize self-care and create time for activities that nourish your body, mind, and soul. Get enough sleep, eat a balanced diet, exercise regularly, and engage in joyful and relaxing activities.

Example: Set aside time each week for activities that help you recharge and unwind, whether it's going for a walk in nature, practicing yoga, or spending time with loved ones.

In summary, building resilience through perseverance and determination requires a combination of mindset, skills, and strategies. By setting clear goals, developing a growth mindset, staying flexible and adaptable, cultivating optimism, developing problem-solving skills, practicing self-compassion, building a strong support network, staying persistent, learning from failure, practicing gratitude, seeking inspiration, and taking care of yourself, you can navigate life's challenges with grace, resilience, and strength. Remember, resilience isn't about avoiding difficulties – it's about facing them head-on with courage and determination, knowing.

Practical Exercises:

Obstacle Identification

Let's take an example of a common problem many people face: feeling overwhelmed by a heavy workload at work. This challenge can affect both personal and professional aspects of life, leading to stress and burnout if not managed effectively. To break down this obstacle into smaller, manageable components, follow these steps:

Identify Specific Tasks

Begin by listing all the tasks and responsibilities that contribute to your heavy workload. It could include project deadlines, daily tasks, meetings, emails, etc.

Prioritize Tasks:

	URGENT	NOT URGENT
IMPORTANT	Quadrant I *urgent and important* DO	Quadrant II *not urgent but important* PLAN
NOT IMPORTANT	Quadrant III *urgent but not important* DELEGATE	Quadrant IV *not urgent and not important* ELIMINATE

Once you have a list, prioritize tasks based on urgency and importance. Use techniques like the Eisenhower Matrix (urgent vs. important) to categorize tasks into four quadrants: urgent and important, important but not urgent, urgent but not important, and neither urgent nor important.

Set Realistic Goals

Set realistic goals for each day or week based on your priorities. Dismantle larger tasks into smaller, actionable steps. It helps create a coherent plan of action and prevents feeling overwhelmed.

Delegate Responsibilities

Identify tasks that can be delegated to others. Delegate tasks based on team members' strengths and workload capacities. Effective delegation not only reduces your workload but also empowers team members.

Effective Time Management

Using the **Pomodoro** Techniques (working in focused intervals with breaks) or time blocking (allocating specific time slots for different tasks) helps maintain focus and productivity.

Seek Resources

Feel free to seek support from colleagues or supervisors if you need help or resources to manage your workload more effectively. Collaborative efforts often lead to innovative solutions and lighten individual burdens.

Practice Self-Care

Finally, prioritize self-care practices such as regular exercise, sufficient sleep, healthy eating habits, and mindfulness activities. Taking good care of your emotional, physical, and mental well-being is helpful for managing stress and staying unbeaten in challenging situations.

By breaking down the obstacle of a heavy workload into these smaller components and implementing strategies to address each component, you can gain clarity, perspective, and a sense of control over your workload, leading to a more balanced and fulfilling life.

Problem-Solving Strategies:

Use problem-solving techniques and apply them to your identified obstacle:

Brainstorming

Brainstorming is a technique where you generate many ideas or solutions in a short amount of time, initially focusing on quantity rather than quality. To apply brainstorming to your heavy workload obstacle, gather a group of trusted colleagues, friends, or family members and start generating ideas on how to manage your workload better. Encourage everyone to contribute freely without judgment and write down all ideas, no matter how unconventional they may seem. After the brainstorming session, review the ideas and identify potential solutions that resonate with you.

Mind Mapping

Mind mapping is a visual technique that helps organize thoughts and ideas in a structured format. To use mind mapping for your obstacle, start by writing down the main problem (e.g., heavy workload) in the center of a blank page. Then, branch out with subtopics such as tasks, priorities, delegation, time management, and self-care. Under each subtopic, jot down related ideas, strategies, or solutions.

This visual representation can help you see connections between different aspects of the problem and generate actionable steps.

Five WHYs Method

The 5 WHYs is a problem-solving technique that involves asking "why" five times to get to the root cause of a problem. To apply the 5 WHYs to your heavy workload obstacle, start by asking yourself why you feel overwhelmed. For example:

- Why am I overwhelmed? Because I have too many tasks to complete.
- Why do I have too many tasks? Because I haven't prioritized them effectively.
- Why haven't I prioritized effectively? Because I don't have a clear system for prioritization.
- Why don't I have a clear system? Because I haven't taken the time to create one.
- Why haven't I taken the time? Because I've been focusing on urgent tasks rather than important ones.

By asking "why" multiple times, you can uncover underlying issues and identify areas where you can make changes to improve the situation.

After applying these problem-solving techniques, you should have a list of potential solutions or strategies to address your heavy workload obstacle. Evaluate each solution based on feasibility, effectiveness, and alignment with your goals and values. Implementing the required strategies can help you overcome the obstacles and achieve a more balanced and manageable workload.

Action Planning

Creating an action plan is a crucial step in addressing any obstacle effectively. Here's a step-by-step guide to help you create an action plan for your identified obstacle (such as a heavy workload):

Define Your Goals

Define your goals that you want to achieve despite any obstacle. For example, your goal could be to manage your workload more efficiently and reduce stress levels.

Identify Specific Steps

Break down your goal into specific, actionable steps. Referencing the strategies and solutions generated earlier (from brainstorming, mind mapping, or the 5 Whys method), list the steps you need to take to address your obstacle. For instance:

Prioritize tasks using the Eisenhower Matrix.

- Delegate and distribute tasks to team members based on their strengths and workload capacities.
- Implement time management techniques like the Pomodoro Technique or time blocking.
- Establish a self-care routine, including regular exercise, sufficient sleep, and mindfulness activities.

Set Timelines

Assign realistic timelines to each step of your action plan. Consider your workload, deadlines, and other commitments when setting timelines. For example:

- Prioritize tasks by the end of the week.
- Delegate tasks by next Monday.
- Start using time management techniques starting tomorrow.
- Incorporate self-care practices daily starting this weekend.

Allocate Resources

Determine what resources you need to implement your action plan successfully. It could include tools (e.g., task management apps, time tracking software), support from colleagues or supervisors, training on prioritization techniques, and access to self-care resources (e.g., gym membership meditation apps).

Monitor Progress

Monitor your progress regularly toward implementing the action plan. Set checkpoints to review your achievements and make any necessary adjustments. Keep track of tasks completed, improvements in workload management, and changes in stress levels.

Stay Flexible

Be open to adjusting your action plan as needed. Circumstances may change, and new challenges or opportunities may arise. Flexibility allows you to adapt your approach while staying focused on your goal.

Celebrate Milestones

Acknowledge and celebrate minor victories along the way. Recognize your progress, no matter how incremental it may seem. Celebrating milestones boosts motivation and reinforces positive behavior.

Commit to Continuous Improvement

Commit to ongoing improvement and learning. Reflect on your action plan to identify what worked well and what could be improved. Incorporate feedback from your experiences and make adjustments for future challenges. By following these steps and committing to taking concrete actions, even if progress is incremental, you can make significant strides in overcoming your obstacle and achieving your goal of managing your workload more effectively. Consistency and perseverance are key to long-term success.

Reflection Questions:

Reflect on a past obstacle or challenge you've overcome.

1. What strategies did you use to navigate through the obstacle?
2. How did you maintain perseverance and determination despite setbacks?

Consider the current obstacle or challenge you identified earlier.

1. Are there any patterns or recurring themes in how you approach obstacles?
2. How can you pull your strengths and resources to overcome this particular challenge?

Think about times when you've encountered unexpected obstacles or setbacks.

1. How did you adapt your plans or strategies in response to these challenges?
2. What did you learn from these experiences?

Reflect on the role of perseverance in building resilience.

1. What motivates you to keep pushing forward when faced with obstacles?
2. How can you cultivate a mindset of determination and resilience in the face of adversity?

Consider seeking support or guidance from mentors, coaches, or trusted friends and family members when facing significant obstacles.

1. How can you leverage their insights and perspectives to overcome challenges more effectively?

By incorporating these practical exercises and reflection questions, you can deepen your understanding of resilience principles and effectively apply them to your own lives. Through problem-solving strategies, action planning, and perseverance, you can overcome obstacles with resilience and determination, ultimately achieving your goals and aspirations.

******

Chapter 5: Cultivating Self-Compassion

"You yourself, as much as anybody in the entire universe, deserve your love and affection." — Buddha

Subunits:

- Exploring the importance of self-compassion.
- Techniques for practicing self-compassion and self-care, including mindfulness and self-acceptance.

Exploring the Importance of Self-compassion.

Self-compassion plays a crucial role in building resilience and well-being by providing a foundation of kindness, understanding, and acceptance toward oneself, especially during difficult times.

Understanding Self-Compassion

Self-compassion involves treating oneself with the same kindness, care, and understanding that one would offer to a good friend. It comprises three major components:

Self-Kindness: Being gentle and understanding with oneself rather than harshly self-critical.

Common Humanity: Recognizing that suffering and setbacks are a natural part of the human experience and that everyone faces challenges at some point.

Mindfulness: Observing one's thoughts and emotions without judgment, allowing for greater self-awareness and emotional resilience.

Importance of Self-Compassion

Self-compassion is essential for building resilience and well-being for several reasons:

Provides Emotional Support

When facing difficulties or setbacks, self-compassion allows individuals to provide themselves with emotional support and comfort, reducing feelings of loneliness and isolation. By offering oneself kindness and understanding, individuals can better cope with stress and adversity. For example, imagine a student who receives a poor grade on an exam. Instead of berating themselves for their perceived failure, they practice self-compassion by acknowledging their efforts, comforting themselves, and recognizing that everyone experiences setbacks in learning.

Reduces Negative Self-Talk

Self-compassion helps to counteract negative self-talk and self-criticism, which can undermine resilience and well-being. By adopting a kinder and more understanding attitude toward oneself, individuals can challenge negative thoughts and beliefs, promoting greater psychological resilience.

For instance, a person who experiences rejection in a romantic relationship may engage in self-critical thoughts, such as "I'm unlovable" or "I'm not good enough." Practicing self-compassion involves responding to these thoughts with kindness and reassurance, such as "It's okay to feel hurt, but I am worthy of love and acceptance."

Promotes Healthy Coping Mechanisms

Self-compassion encourages individuals to engage in healthy coping mechanisms when facing challenges, such as seeking social support, practicing mindfulness, or engaging in self-care activities. By nurturing oneself with kindness and understanding, individuals can develop more effective strategies for managing stress and adversity.

For example, a person experiencing work-related stress may practice self-compassion by taking breaks when needed, seeking support from colleagues or friends, and engaging in stress-reducing activities like exercise or meditation.

Fosters Resilience and Adaptability

Self-compassion fosters resilience by promoting a mindset of acceptance and adaptability in the face of adversity. Rather than dwelling on past mistakes or failures, individuals who practice self-compassion are more likely to learn from their experiences, bounce back from setbacks, and persevere in the pursuit of their goals.

For instance, a business owner who experiences a financial setback may practice self-compassion by acknowledging their disappointment and seeking guidance from mentors or financial advisors. By approaching the situation with kindness and understanding, they can develop a new strategy for overcoming the setback and moving forward with resilience.

Research Supporting Self-Compassion

Numerous studies have demonstrated the benefits of self-compassion for resilience and well-being. For example, a study published in the Journal of Personality and Social Psychology found that self-compassion was positively associated with psychological well-being, including greater happiness, life satisfaction, and positive mood.

Source: Neff, K. D., & Vonk, R. (2009). Self-compassion versus global self-esteem: Two different ways of relating to oneself. Journal of Personality, 77(1), 23-50.

Another study published in the Journal of Clinical Psychology found that self-compassion was negatively associated with symptoms of depression, anxiety, and stress, highlighting its protective role against mental health problems.

Source: MacBeth, A., & Gumley, A. (2012). Exploring compassion: A meta-analysis of the association between self-compassion and psychopathology. Clinical Psychology Review, 32(6), 545-552.

These findings underscore the importance of self-compassion in promoting resilience, well-being, and psychological health across various contexts.

Practical Strategies for Cultivating Self-Compassion

There are several practical strategies individuals can use to cultivate self-compassion in their daily lives:

Practice Self-Kindness

Treat yourself with kindness and understanding, especially during difficult times. Offer yourself words of encouragement, comfort, and reassurance as you would to a good friend.

Validate Your Feelings

Acknowledge and validate your feelings without judgment or criticism. Allow yourself to experience emotions such as sadness, anger, or fear, recognizing that they are a natural part of the human experience.

Practice Mindfulness

Cultivate mindfulness by observing your thoughts and emotions without attachment or judgment. Practice techniques such as meditation, deep breathing, or body scanning to increase self-awareness and emotional resilience.

Challenge Self-Critical Thoughts

Challenge negative self-talk and self-critical thoughts by questioning their accuracy and validity. Replace self-criticism with more balanced and compassionate perspectives.

Seek Social Support

Reach out to friends, family members, or support groups for emotional support and validation during challenging times. Share your experiences and feelings with others who can offer empathy and understanding.

Engage in Self-Care

Prioritize self-care activities that nurture your physical, emotional, and mental well-being. Take time for activities you enjoy, such as hobbies, exercise, or spending time in nature.

Practice Gratitude

Cultivate an attitude of gratitude by focusing on the things you're thankful for in your life. Keep a gratitude journal or take time each day to reflect on the positive aspects of your day.

In conclusion, self-compassion is a powerful tool for building resilience and well-being, providing a foundation of kindness, understanding, and acceptance toward oneself during difficult times. By practicing self-compassion, individuals can provide themselves with emotional support, reduce negative self-talk, promote healthy coping mechanisms, and foster resilience in the face of adversity. Through practical strategies such as self-kindness, mindfulness, and seeking social support, individuals can cultivate self-compassion and harness its benefits for greater resilience and well-being.

Techniques for practicing self-compassion and self-care.

Practicing self-compassion and self-care, including mindfulness and self-acceptance, is essential for promoting emotional well-being and resilience.

Self-Compassion

Self-compassion involves treating oneself with kindness, understanding, and acceptance, especially during times of difficulty or suffering. It has three key components:

Self-Kindness: Being gentle and understanding with oneself rather than harshly self-critical.

Common Humanity: Recognizing that suffering and setbacks are a natural part of the human experience and that everyone faces challenges at some point.

Mindfulness: Observing one's thoughts and emotions without judgment, allowing for greater self-awareness and emotional resilience.

For example, imagine you've made a mistake at work and are feeling disappointed in yourself. Instead of criticizing yourself for your perceived failure, you practice self-compassion by acknowledging your efforts, comforting yourself, and recognizing that everyone makes mistakes from time to time.

Self-Care

Self-care involves prioritizing activities and practices that nurture your physical, emotional, and mental well-being. It's about taking deliberate steps to care for yourself and replenish your energy reserves.

Some self-care practices include getting enough sleep, eating nutritious foods, exercising regularly, spending time outdoors, engaging in hobbies or activities you enjoy, and setting boundaries to protect your time and energy.

Mindfulness

Mindfulness is the practice of paying attention to the present moment without judgment, allowing you to cultivate greater awareness and acceptance of your thoughts, emotions, and experiences.

You can practice mindfulness by focusing on your breath, observing sensations in your body, or simply being fully present in whatever activity you're engaged in, whether it's eating, walking, or talking to a friend.

Self-Acceptance

Self-acceptance involves embracing oneself fully, including both strengths and weaknesses, without judgment or criticism. It's about acknowledging and embracing your authentic self, flaws and all.

Instead of striving for perfection or comparing yourself to others, you practice self-acceptance by recognizing your unique qualities, strengths, and talents and accepting yourself just as you are. Practicing Self-Compassion and Self-Care

Now, let's explore some specific techniques for practicing self-compassion and self-care, including mindfulness and self-acceptance:

Loving-Kindness Meditation

Loving-kindness meditation is a practice that involves cultivating feelings of love, compassion, and goodwill towards oneself and others. You can practice loving-kindness meditation by silently repeating phrases such as "May I be happy, may I be healthy, may I be safe, may I be at ease" while focusing on feelings of warmth and kindness towards yourself.

Sit quietly in a comfortable position, close your eyes, and begin by directing loving-kindness towards yourself.

Repeat the phrases **"May I be happy, may I be healthy, may I be safe, may I be at ease"** while visualizing yourself surrounded by love and compassion.

Self-Compassion Break

The self-compassion break is a simple technique developed by Dr. Kristin Neff, a leading researcher in self-compassion. It involves pausing for a moment during times of difficulty to acknowledge your suffering, remind yourself that suffering is a natural part of life, and offer yourself words of kindness and comfort.

When you're feeling overwhelmed or stressed, take a moment to pause and place your hand over your heart. Acknowledge your feelings of distress and say to yourself, **"This is a moment of suffering. Suffering is a part of life. May I be kind to myself at this moment, and may I give myself the compassion I need?"**

Body Scan Meditation

Body scan meditation is a mindfulness practice that involves systematically scanning your body from head to toe, paying attention to any sensations or feelings you notice without judgment. This practice can help you develop greater body awareness and cultivate a sense of presence and relaxation.

Find a quiet, comfortable space to sit or lie down. Close your eyes and focus on your breath for a few moments. Then, slowly begin scanning your body from head to toe, noticing any areas of tension, discomfort, or relaxation. Observe these sensations without trying to change them, allowing yourself to be fully present in your body.

Gratitude Journaling

Gratitude journaling involves writing down things you're grateful for regularly, whether it's once a day, once a week, or whenever you feel inspired. Keeping a gratitude journal can help shift your focus away from negativity and towards the positive aspects of your life, fostering feelings of appreciation and contentment. Please take a few minutes each day to write down three things you're grateful for, whether it's a beautiful sunset, a kind gesture from a friend, or a delicious meal. Reflect on these blessings and notice how they make you feel.

Positive affirmations for a powerful impact

Affirmations are positive statements or phrases that you repeat to yourself to reinforce a positive belief or mindset. Affirmations can help challenge negative self-talk and cultivate self-compassion and self-acceptance. Choose affirmations that resonate with you, such as:

"I am worthy of love and acceptance,"

"I trust myself to handle whatever comes my way," or

"I am enough just as I am."

Repeat these affirmations to yourself regularly, either silently or out loud, to reinforce positive beliefs about yourself.

Source References / Citations:

Neff, K. D., & Germer, C. K. (2013). A pilot study and randomized controlled trial of the mindful self-compassion program. Journal of Clinical Psychology, 69(1), 28-44.

Neff, K. D., Kirkpatrick, K. L., & Rude, S. S. (2007). Self-compassion and adaptive psychological functioning. Journal of Research in Personality, 41(1), 139-154.

These studies provide evidence for the effectiveness of self-compassion and mindfulness-based interventions in promoting emotional well-being and resilience. By incorporating these techniques into your daily routine, you can cultivate greater self-compassion, self-care, and well-being, leading to a more fulfilling and resilient life.

Reflection Questions

1. Reflect on your own self-talk and inner dialogue. Are you typically self-critical or compassionate towards yourself during difficult times? How does this impact your resilience and well-being?
2. Consider a recent challenge or setback you've faced. How did you respond to yourself in that moment? Were you able to offer yourself kindness and understanding, or did you engage in self-blame and criticism?
3. Think about times when you've offered compassion and support to others. How can you extend the same level of kindness and care to yourself during times of struggle or hardship?
4. Reflect on the connection between self-compassion and resilience. How does treating yourself with compassion and understanding contribute to your ability to bounce back from adversity and navigate life's ups and downs?
5. Consider incorporating self-compassion practices such as mindfulness, self-acceptance, and loving-kindness into your daily routine. How can you prioritize self-care and cultivate a greater sense of compassion towards yourself moving forward?

Chapter 6: Thriving With Determination

"Be steadfast in your determination, like a rock facing the crashing waves."

Subunits:

- Long-term benefits of resilience in personal and professional growth.

- Strategies for thriving in the face of adversity and achieving success

- Cultivating resilience for a meaningful life journey.

Resilience for personal and professional growth.

Examining the long-term benefits of resilience in personal and professional growth reveals how individuals who cultivate resilience can thrive despite facing adversity.

Personal Growth:

Resilience plays a crucial role in personal growth by enabling individuals to overcome challenges, adapt to change, and develop greater self-awareness and emotional strength. Here are some long-term benefits of resilience in personal growth:

Increased Emotional Wellness

Resilient people are better prepared to manage their stress, cope with challenges and setbacks, and maintain a positive outlook on life. Over time, this can lead to greater emotional well-being and overall happiness.

Example: Consider someone who faces a series of setbacks in their personal life, such as the loss of a loved one, financial difficulties, or health problems. Through resilience, they are able to navigate these challenges, find meaning in their experiences, and emerge stronger and more resilient than before.

Enhanced Problem-Solving Skills

Resilient individuals develop strong problem-solving skills through their ability to adapt and overcome obstacles. Over time, this can lead to greater confidence and competence in navigating life's challenges.

Example: A student who struggles academically may initially feel overwhelmed by their difficulties. However, through resilience, they learn to seek help when needed, develop effective study strategies, and ultimately achieve academic success.

Greater Self-Confidence

Resilience fosters a sense of self-efficacy and belief in one's ability to overcome adversity. As individuals face and overcome challenges, they build confidence in their capacity to handle future difficulties.

Example: A professional who faces rejection in their career may initially feel discouraged. However, through resilience, they persevere in their efforts, learn from their experiences, and ultimately achieve success in their chosen field.

Improved Relationships

Resilient individuals are better able to navigate interpersonal conflicts, communicate effectively, and maintain healthy relationships. Over time, this can lead to deeper connections and more fulfilling relationships with others.

Example: A couple faces a significant challenge in their relationship, such as financial strain or a communication breakdown. Through resilience, they work together to address the issue, communicate openly and honestly, and strengthen their bond as a result.

Professional Growth

In addition to personal growth, resilience also contributes to professional growth by enabling individuals to thrive in their careers despite facing setbacks and challenges. Here are some long-term benefits of resilience in professional growth:

Increased Job Satisfaction

Individuals with determination are better equipped to handle the pressures and demands of the workplace, leading to greater job satisfaction and fulfillment.

Example: A professional faces a high-stress work environment with tight deadlines and demanding clients. Through resilience, they remain calm under pressure, prioritize tasks effectively, and ultimately find satisfaction in their work despite the challenges.

Enhanced Leadership Skills:

Resilient individuals make effective leaders by inspiring and motivating others, navigating uncertainty and change, and fostering a culture of resilience within their teams or organizations.

Example: A manager faces a period of organizational change, such as a restructuring or merger. Through resilience, they lead their team through the transition, provide support and guidance, and ultimately help their team adapt and thrive in the new environment.

Improved Problem-Solving Abilities

Resilient individuals excel at problem-solving by approaching challenges with creativity, flexibility, and determination. Over time, this can lead to greater innovation and success in the workplace.

Example: An entrepreneur faces a setback in their business, such as a product launch failure or a loss of funding. Through resilience, they pivot their strategy, learn from their mistakes, and ultimately achieve success through innovation and perseverance.

Better Career Opportunities

Resilient people are more likely to bounce back from setbacks, leading to greater career advancement and opportunities for growth, and realize their career goals.

Example: A professional faces a setback in their career, such as a job loss or a failed project. Through resilience, they leverage their skills and experiences, network effectively, and ultimately secure new and better job opportunities.

Source References / Citations:

While there may not be specific studies directly linking resilience to long-term personal and professional growth, various research and literature support the connection between resilience and positive outcomes in both domains.

1. Masten, A. S. (2001). Ordinary magic: Resilience processes in development. American Psychologist, 56(3), 227-238.

   This article explores resilience processes in development, highlighting how resilience contributes to positive outcomes in various life domains, including personal and professional growth.

2. Luthar, S. S., Cicchetti, D., & Becker, B. (2000).

a. The construct of resilience: Child Development, 71(3), 543-562.

This paper provides a critical evaluation of the construct of resilience and offers guidelines for future research. It emphasizes the importance of resilience in promoting positive development and well-being across the lifespan.

Resilience plays a critical role in promoting long-term personal and professional growth by enabling individuals to overcome challenges, adapt to change, and thrive despite adversity. By cultivating resilience, individuals can experience greater emotional well-being, enhanced problem-solving skills, improved relationships, increased job satisfaction, enhanced leadership abilities, and better career opportunities. Through resilience, individuals can navigate life's ups and downs with confidence, resilience, and, ultimately, success.

Strategies for Thriving in Adversity and Achieving Success

Strategies for thriving in the face of adversity and using resilience as a foundation for success involve cultivating a growth mindset, practicing self-compassion, seeking social support, engaging in resilience-building activities, setting realistic goals, accepting failure as a learning opportunity, cultivating optimism, and adapting to change. By incorporating these strategies into their lives, individuals can develop greater resilience, overcome challenges, and achieve their goals with confidence and determination.

Develop a Growth Mindset

Believing in a growth mindset involves developing abilities and intelligence through dedication and effort. It means seeing challenges as chances to grow and learn rather than as impossible barriers.

Example: Instead of giving up when faced with a difficult task, approach it with curiosity and determination, seeing it as a chance to improve your skills and abilities.

Cultivate Self-Compassion

Self-compassion involves treating oneself with kindness, understanding, and acceptance, especially during times of difficulty or suffering. By practicing self-compassion, individuals can provide themselves with emotional support and comfort, reducing feelings of stress and anxiety.

Example: Instead of criticizing yourself for making a mistake, learn to acknowledge their efforts, offer yourself words of encouragement, and remind yourself that everyone makes mistakes.

Seek Social Support

Building a strong support network of friends, family members, and mentors can provide invaluable emotional support and practical assistance during challenging times. Seeking support from others can help individuals feel less alone and more capable of facing adversity.

For example, when facing a difficult situation, seek support from a trusted friend or family member for timely advice, guidance, or simply lending you a listening ear.

Practice Resilience-Building Activities

Taking up activities such as mindfulness, meditation, journaling, or physical exercise can help individuals develop greater emotional strength and coping skills. These activities can also provide a sense of calm and relaxation during times of stress.

Practice mindfulness meditation regularly to cultivate an awareness of your thoughts and emotions, which will help you respond to challenges with greater clarity and resilience.

Set Realistic Goals

Allowing individuals to set realistic and achievable goals enables them to effectively focus their efforts and resources, thereby increasing their chances of success. By breaking larger goals down into smaller, manageable steps, individuals can maintain motivation and momentum.

Example: Instead of aiming to run a marathon with no prior training, someone might set a goal to run a certain distance each week, escalating their mileage.

Embrace Failure as a Learning Opportunity

Viewing failure as a natural and necessary part of the learning process can help individuals develop resilience and perseverance. By considering failure as a chance to learn, grow, and improve, individuals can bounce back from setbacks with renewed determination and resilience.

Instead of giving up after experiencing a setback, reflect on where you went wrong, identify areas for improvement, and use that knowledge to approach the situation differently in the future.

Cultivate Optimism

Maintaining a positive outlook and focusing on the potential for growth and success can help individuals remain determined in the face of adversity. Optimistic individuals are better able to see setbacks as temporary and surmountable rather than as permanent failures.

Instead of dwelling on past failures, focus on your strengths, skills, and past successes, believing that you can overcome future challenges.

Adapt to Change

Flexibility and adaptability are essential qualities for thriving in the face of adversity. By embracing change and being willing to adjust their plans and strategies as needed, individuals can boldly face uncertain or challenging situations with greater ease and resilience.

When faced with unexpected changes in their circumstances, they assess the situation objectively, identify potential opportunities or advantages, and adapt their approach accordingly.

Cultivating Resilience for a Meaningful Life Journey.

Encouraging individuals to continue cultivating resilience as an ongoing practice is crucial for fostering a fulfilling and meaningful life journey. Resilience is not just a trait; it's a skill that can be developed and strengthened.

Encouraging individuals to continue cultivating resilience as an ongoing practice is essential for fostering a fulfilling and meaningful life journey. By accepting challenges as opportunities for growth, adopting a growth mindset, practicing self-compassion and self-care, building supportive relationships, and celebrating progress and successes, individuals can develop greater resilience and thrive in the face of adversity. Through ongoing effort and practice, resilience can become a guiding force that enables individuals to conquer challenges and obstacles, achieve their goals, and lead fulfilling lives.

Understanding Resilience as a Lifelong Journey

Resilience is the ability to adapt and bounce back from adversity, challenges, and setbacks. It's about facing life's difficulties with courage, perseverance, and optimism. While some individuals may naturally possess greater resilience than others, it's important to recognize that resilience is not fixed; it can be cultivated and nurtured throughout one's life.

Example: Consider a person who experiences a series of setbacks in their career, such as job loss, rejection, or failure. Instead of giving up, they persistently seek new opportunities, learn from their experiences, and ultimately achieve success. This resilience didn't happen overnight but was developed through ongoing effort and practice.

Source: Masten, A. S. (2001). Ordinary magic: Resilience processes in development. American Psychologist, 56(3), 227-238.

Embracing Challenges as Opportunities for Growth

Encouraging individuals to view challenges and obstacles as opportunities for growth and learning is essential for fostering resilience. Rather than being overwhelmed by difficulties, resilient individuals see them as chances to develop new skills, gain valuable insights, and become stronger and more capable in the process.

Example: Imagine a student who struggles with a particularly challenging subject in school. Instead of avoiding it or giving up, they seek out additional resources, ask for help from teachers or peers, and persistently practice until they improve. In doing so, they not only master the subject but also develop resilience and confidence in their abilities.

Source: Duckworth, A. L. (2016). Grit: The power of passion and perseverance. Scribner.

Cultivating a Growth Mindset

Encouraging individuals to adopt a growth mindset, wherein they believe that their abilities and intelligence can be developed through effort and practice, is crucial for building resilience. By embracing challenges, learning from failures, and persisting in the face of setbacks, individuals with a growth mindset can develop greater resilience and achieve their goals.

Example: A person who faces rejection in their job search might initially feel discouraged. However, instead of viewing it as a reflection of their abilities, they see it as an opportunity to learn and grow. They seek feedback, identify areas for improvement, and persistently apply for new opportunities until they succeed.

Source: Dweck, C. S. (2006). Mindset: The new psychology of success. Random House.

Practicing Self-Compassion and Self-Care

Encouraging individuals to practice self-compassion and self-care is essential for maintaining resilience over the long term. Self-compassion involves treating oneself with kindness, understanding, and acceptance, especially during times of difficulty or suffering. Self-care involves prioritizing activities that nurture one's physical, emotional, and mental well-being.

Example: A person who experiences a setback in their personal life, such as a breakup or loss of a loved one, might feel overwhelmed by grief and sadness. By practicing self-compassion, they offer themselves words of kindness and comfort, seek support from friends, and practice relaxation.

Building and Maintaining Supportive Relationships

Encouraging individuals to build and maintain supportive relationships with friends, family members, mentors, and peers is crucial for fostering resilience. Having a strong support network provides emotional support, practical assistance, and a sense of belonging, all of which are essential for coping with life's challenges.

Example: A person who faces a significant challenge in their life, such as a health crisis or financial difficulty, might turn to their friends and family for support. By sharing their struggles, seeking advice, and receiving encouragement, they feel less alone and more capable of overcoming adversity.

Source: Cohen, S., & Wills, T. A. (1985). Stress, social support, and the buffering hypothesis. Psychological Bulletin, 98(2), 310-357.

Celebrating Progress and Successes

Encouraging individuals to celebrate their progress and successes, no matter how small, is important for maintaining motivation and resilience. By acknowledging their achievements and reflecting on how far they've come, individuals can stay focused, optimistic, and resilient in the face of future challenges.

Example: A person who sets a goal for themselves, such as completing a marathon or learning a new skill, might celebrate each milestone along the way.

Source: Fredrickson, B. L. (2004). The broaden-and-build theory of positive emotions. Philosophical Transactions of the Royal Society of London. Series B: Biological Sciences, 359(1449), 1367-1378.

Reflection Questions:

1. Reflect on your personal and professional growth journey. How has resilience contributed to your achievements and successes? What strengths or qualities have helped you thrive in the face of adversity?
2. Consider the goals you've set for yourself in various areas of your life. How can you use resilience as a foundation for pursuing these goals with determination and perseverance?
3. Think about a recent challenge or setback you've faced. How did you respond to the situation, and what did you learn from the experience? How can you apply these lessons to future challenges and opportunities?
4. Reflect on the concept of thriving through resilience. What does thriving mean to you, and how do you envision resilience contributing to your ability to thrive in all aspects of your life?
5. Consider the importance of cultivating resilience as an ongoing practice. How can you integrate resilience-building exercises and principles into your daily routine to support a fulfilling and meaningful life journey?

By practicing reflection, you can deepen your understanding of resilience and apply it to your lives effectively.

Through goal setting, strengths identification, and ongoing resilience practices, you can create a fulfilling and meaningful life journey grounded in resilience.

Disclaimer

This book, 'Master Creative Thinking' is intended to inspire and empower readers to enhance their creative potential and achieve success. It explores various aspects of creative thinking, including its definition, significance, and its role in attaining success in different endeavors. Throughout the book, numerous examples of successful individuals who have utilized creative thinking to realize their dreams are provided for illustrative purposes. Additionally, references to online apps, opportunities, and platforms such as Amazon, Google, Medium, and Fiverr, among others, are mentioned solely to provide readers with resources and tools that may help in their creative journey.

It is important to note that including these examples and references is not intended as a promotion or endorsement of any specific product, service, or platform. The author does not have any financial interests or gains associated with the mentioned entities. Readers are encouraged to evaluate the information presented in this book critically and to conduct their research before making any decisions or investments. The author shall not be held liable for any consequences arising from the use of the information provided herein. This disclaimer serves to clarify the intentions behind the content of this book and to ensure transparency and integrity in its presentation.

Overview of "Master Your Learning Styles" - the second book in the Cognitive Mastery Series.

"Master Your Learning Styles: Unleash Your Potential Through Neuroscience" promises a transformation of self-discovery and empowerment by diving deep into the fascinating world of learning styles. This book, authored with a blend of cutting-edge neuroscience research and practical insights, aims to guide readers in understanding their unique learning preferences and leveraging them to excel in various learning environments.

The primary purpose of "Master Your Learning Style" is to demystify the concept of learning styles and emphasize their crucial role in optimizing learning experiences. By unraveling common myths and misconceptions, the book sets the stage for readers to appreciate the diversity in how individuals process and retain information. This understanding serves as a foundation for readers to harness their preferred learning styles effectively.

One of the significant benefits for readers is gaining clarity on their preferred learning modes, whether they lean towards visual, auditory, kinesthetic, social, solitary, verbal, logical-mathematical, or naturalistic learning styles. Armed with this knowledge, readers can tailor their learning strategies to align with their strengths, resulting in improved comprehension, retention, and overall academic or professional success.

The book's insights and practical strategies are designed to benefit readers across various aspects of life. For students, understanding their learning styles can lead to more effective study techniques, better exam performance, and a deeper engagement with the learning material. Professionals can leverage their learning styles to enhance productivity, problem-solving abilities, and job performance. Lifelong learners will appreciate how aligning their learning approaches with their preferences can make learning more enjoyable, sustainable, and fulfilling.

Moreover, "Master Your Learning Style" goes beyond academic or professional settings. It acknowledges the holistic nature of learning and how it extends to personal growth and self-improvement. By embracing their preferred learning styles, readers can cultivate lifelong learning habits, enhance critical thinking skills, and foster a growth mindset that is essential for success in all areas of life.

The book's emphasis on neuroscience adds a layer of scientific understanding, helping readers appreciate the cognitive mechanisms behind different learning styles. This knowledge not only enhances self-awareness but also empowers readers to make the right decisions about their learning strategies, study environments, and learning resources.

"Master Your Learning Style" encourages readers to view learning as a continuous journey rather than a static destination. By embracing lifelong learning and adaptability, readers can stay ahead in an ever-evolving world, acquire new skills, and navigate challenges with confidence and resilience.

In essence, this book is a valuable resource for anyone looking to unlock their full learning potential, whether they are students, professionals, or lifelong learners. By understanding and embracing their unique learning styles, readers can embark on a fulfilling journey of growth, knowledge acquisition, and personal development. So dive into "Master Your Learning Style" and embark on a path towards mastering the art of learning for success in all aspects of life.

******

Reference

1. https://www.brainyquote.com
2. https://www.goodreads.com/work/quotes
3. https://buildd.co/product/id-fresh-food-success-story
4. https://opentextbc.ca/introductiontopsychology/chapter/3-2-our-brains-control-our-thoughts-feelings-and behavior.
5. Wikipedia
6. https://opentextbc.ca/introductiontopsychology/chapter/3-2-our-brains-control-our-thoughts-feelings-and-behavior
7. https://olgareinholdt.com/2023/05/26/rethinking-responsibility-moving-beyond-guilt-and-embracing-agency/
8. https://doi.org/10.21067/jip.v11i2.5908.
9. , https://doi.org/10.1108/jeee-08-2022-0232.
10. Embed. https://slides.com/crossingborderseducation/implicit-bias/embed?style=light&byline=hidden&share=hidden
11. https://www.motivationiseverything.com/on-mindset/the-power-of-mindset-unleashing-your-power-within/

12. https://mindlifetv.com/entrepreneurs/gates-foundation-ceo-defends-philanthropys-influence-on-global-health/
13. https://www.mic.com/culture/serena-williams-evolution-leaving-tennis
14. https://www.teachingexpertise.com/classroom-ideas/stem-books/
15. https://lantanarecovery.com/the-benefits-of-art-therapy-in-addiction-recovery/
16. https://pdflake.com/creative-confidence-pdf-book-in-english-by-tom-and-david-kelley/
17. https://www.thecomplexmedia.com/theater-broadways-biggest-hits-a-guide-to-the-best-musicals-of-the-past-decade/
18. https://yourstory.com/2023/07/malavika-hegde-ccd-debt-turnaround-story
19. https://innovativezoneindia.com/meet-ips-officer-manoj-kumar-sharma/
20. https://www.mariposasources.com/post/growth-mindset
21. Dweck, C. S. (2006). Mindset: The new psychology of success. Random House.
22. Cohen, S., & Wills, T. A. (1985). Stress, social support, and the buffering hypothesis. Psychological Bulletin, 98(2), 310-357.

23. Dweck, C. S. (2006). Mindset: The new psychology of success. Random House.
24. Seligman, M. E. P. (2006). Learned optimism. Vintage.
25. https://etherapypro.com/building-resilience-transform-life/
26. Niederman, Fred, and Salvatore March. "Moving the Work System Theory Forward." Journal of the Association for Information Systems, vol. 15, no. 6, 2014, pp. 346-360.
27. Tamara Katarina Mantiri, Tamara Katarina Mantiri. "Perancangan Buku Informasi Self-Compassion." 2022, https://core.ac.uk/download/535036974.pdf.
28. https://www.mindful.org/the-transformative-effects-of-mindful-self-compassion/

******

Printed in the USA
CPSIA information can be obtained
at www.ICGtesting.com
CBHW051325200724
11806CB00044B/533